MAKING FACES

Peter Firmin

COLLINS ORIGINAL
PICTURE LIONS

This book will show you how to make some very simple puppets out of things you'll find around the house.

Keep a large cardboard box handy to hold useful things like these: empty boxes, bottle tops, egg boxes (especially the sort made of pressed paper called papier mâché), buttons, scraps of felt and furry cloth, metal foil, paper plates, paper dishes, bottle corks, thin wire coat hangers, beads, string and wool, drinking straws, toilet-roll tubes, and empty plastic film cans. Don't throw away any worn out socks, jumpers or gloves; they are just the things to start off a puppet.

The glue to use is called PVA. Sometimes it is used for woodworking, and is also called 'school' glue.

These puppets don't take long to make, and with a grown-up to help you cut, sew and work out the more difficult pieces, there will soon be enough characters for you and your friends to have fun with.

First published in the U.K. 1988 by
Picture Lions,
8 Grafton Street, London W1X 3LA

Picture Lions is an imprint of the Children's Division,
part of the Collins Publishing Group.

Copyright © Peter Firmin 1988

Printed in Great Britain
by Warners (Midlands) plc, Bourne and London

A TALKING ANIMAL

Find an old jersey or sock. Fold inside the end of the sleeve or the toe and pin round with six safety pins.

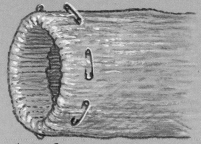

EARS

Push in two large flat buttons or coins. At about 10 cms from the end, pull the wool tight around them and fix with rubber bands or safety pins.

Put your fingers inside, around the mouth. Hold the neck in place with a rubber band.

EYES

Sew or pin on buttons.

What sort of animal is it?
This one has horns made of rolled-up paper.
She is called Old Jersey Cow.

PUSSY FOOT An old sock cat

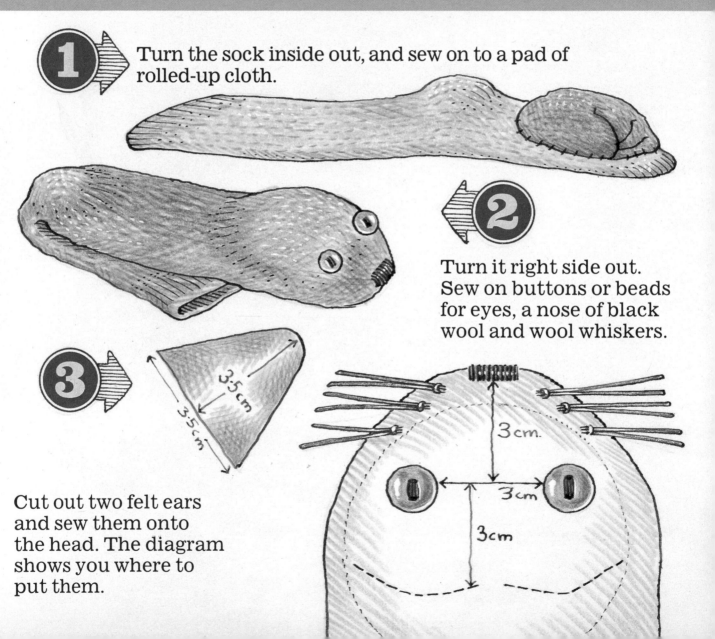

1 Turn the sock inside out, and sew on to a pad of rolled-up cloth.

2 Turn it right side out. Sew on buttons or beads for eyes, a nose of black wool and wool whiskers.

3 Cut out two felt ears and sew them onto the head. The diagram shows you where to put them.

3·5 cm
3·5 cm

3 cm.
3 cm
3 cm

4 Cut out a felt mouth and tongue.

Fold the mouth shape and sew the tongue into it. Sew or glue the mouth below the nose. It is easier if you put your hand inside the sock.

Can you make her tail and paws? Use an old stocking for these.

6cm 4cm

3cm

3cm

RATTLE SNAKE A string puppet

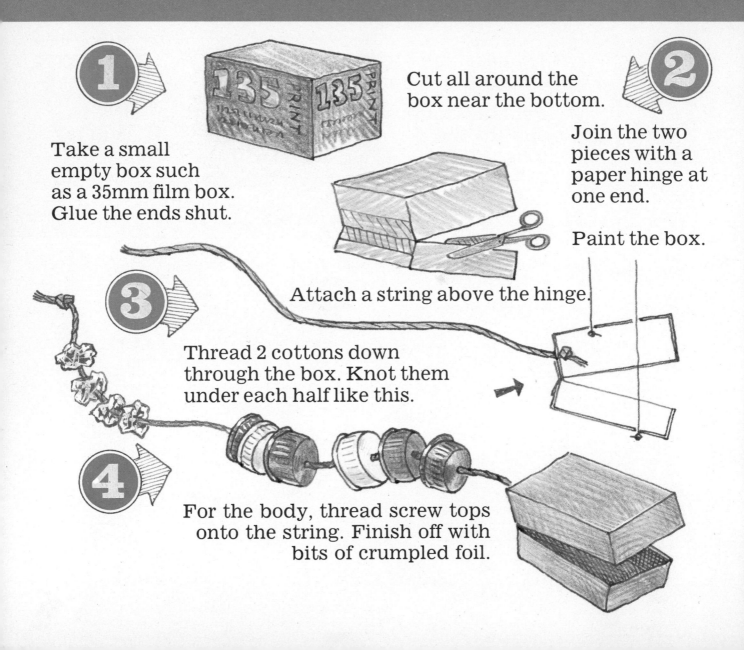

1 Take a small empty box such as a 35mm film box. Glue the ends shut.

2 Cut all around the box near the bottom.

Join the two pieces with a paper hinge at one end.

Paint the box.

Attach a string above the hinge.

3 Thread 2 cottons down through the box. Knot them under each half like this.

4 For the body, thread screw tops onto the string. Finish off with bits of crumpled foil.

You will need: a small box, glue, scissors, paper tape, paint, string, cotton, metal and plastic screw tops, kitchen foil, two straws, modelling clay.

5 Thread a piece of string through one and a half straws. Knot it at both ends.

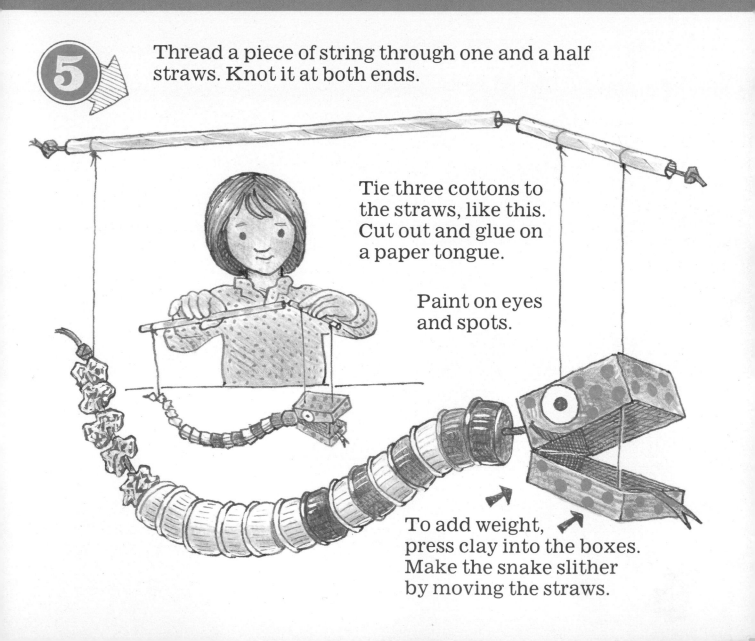

Tie three cottons to the straws, like this. Cut out and glue on a paper tongue.

Paint on eyes and spots.

To add weight, press clay into the boxes. Make the snake slither by moving the straws.

MATCHBOX CLOWN
A rod puppet

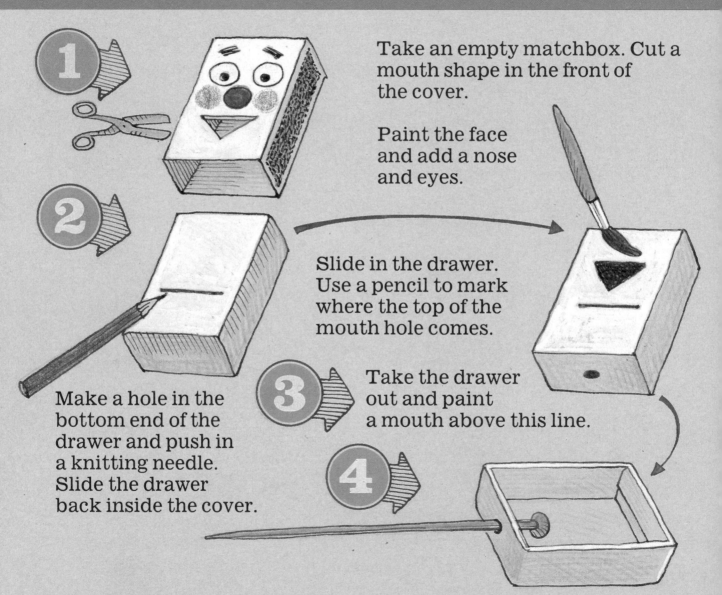

1 Take an empty matchbox. Cut a mouth shape in the front of the cover.

Paint the face and add a nose and eyes.

2 Slide in the drawer. Use a pencil to mark where the top of the mouth hole comes.

Make a hole in the bottom end of the drawer and push in a knitting needle. Slide the drawer back inside the cover.

3 Take the drawer out and paint a mouth above this line.

4

You will need: an empty matchbow, glue, scissors, paint, a
knitting needle or thin cane, thin wood or
thick card, a rubber band, tissue or crepe paper.

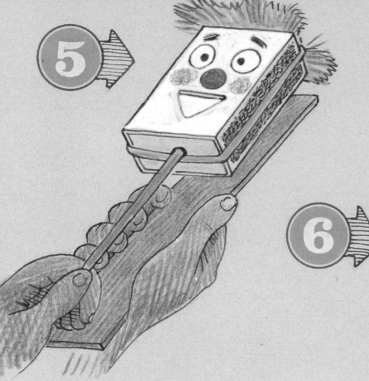

5

6

Glue a strip of wood or thick
card to the back.
Put a rubber band around the
box and tuck in wool for hair.

Make a coat of tissue or crepe
paper. Glue it to the back and
sides of the box and wrap it
around the front. Cut out and
glue on paper arms. Make a hat
out of a piece of egg box. Hold the
strip of wood and pull down the
needle to make the clown talk.

MR CHATTERBOX A rod puppet

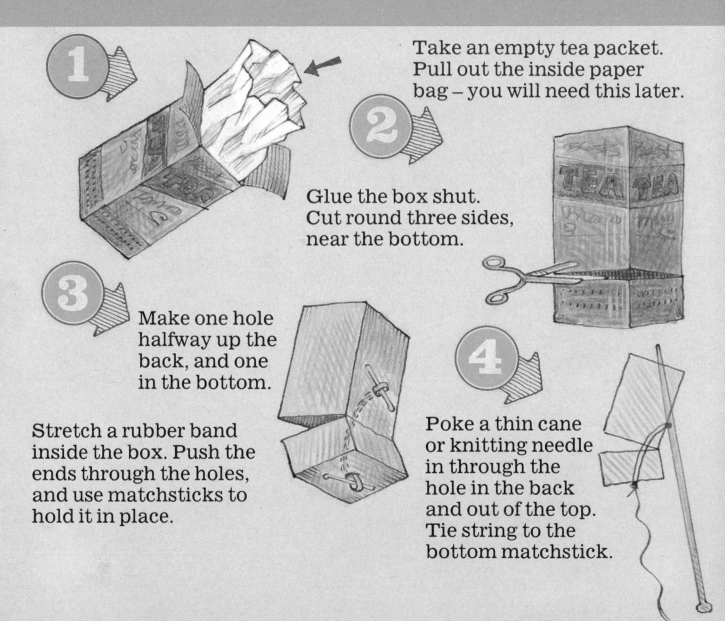

1 Take an empty tea packet. Pull out the inside paper bag – you will need this later.

2 Glue the box shut. Cut round three sides, near the bottom.

3 Make one hole halfway up the back, and one in the bottom.

Stretch a rubber band inside the box. Push the ends through the holes, and use matchsticks to hold it in place.

4 Poke a thin cane or knitting needle in through the hole in the back and out of the top. Tie string to the bottom matchstick.

Cut a cork in half and then one half into quarters. Glue the pieces on for ears and a nose.

5

6

When the glue is dry, paint the face, eyes and hair.

Use the paper bag as a hat, or make your own.
Make a crepe paper coat and glue it to the back of the head.
Cut out and stick on paper arms.

Pull the string to make him chatter.

DIZZY DUCK A hand puppet

 **These are the eyes.**

Cut an egg box, leaving only two bumps fixed to the lid. Glue the lid and base together.

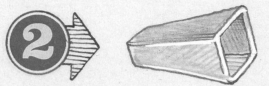 Cut a thimble shape from the inside of an egg box, or make a paper tube to fit your finger.

3cm

 For the beak, fold the paper plate in half. Glue the thimble shape to the plate and then the beak to the eyes.

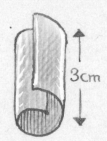

Glue the thimble shape here.

Press onto egg box bumps.

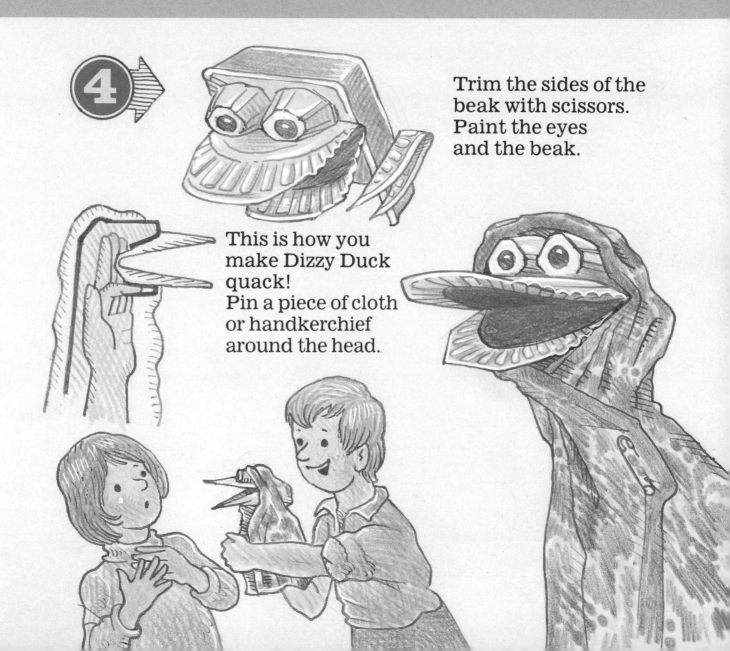

4 ➡

Trim the sides of the beak with scissors. Paint the eyes and the beak.

This is how you make Dizzy Duck quack! Pin a piece of cloth or handkerchief around the head.

CREEPING CATERPILLAR

 **1** Cut a square of furry cloth or wool. Sew the long sides together to make a tube.

13cm

10cm

 **2** Put a cork into each end. Make one stick out – this is the head. Push the other one right inside. Glue both in place.

3

Ask a grown-up to cut one side from a coat hanger and bend each end up like this.

You will need: some furry cloth or wool, scissors, needle and cotton, glue, two corks, a thin wire coat hanger, wire cutters, paint, coloured wool.

4

Make a hole in each cork, poke in the ends of the wire and glue them in place. Make the caterpillar creep along the back of a chair or table by squeezing the wires together.

Paint the face, adding the eyes and mouth. Sew tufts of wool along the back.

5

DREADFUL DRAGON

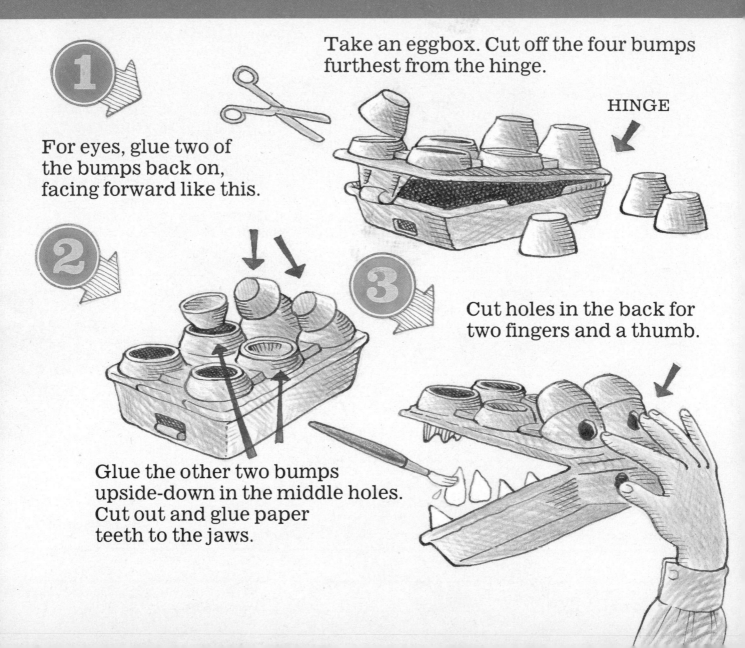

1 Take an eggbox. Cut off the four bumps furthest from the hinge.

HINGE

For eyes, glue two of the bumps back on, facing forward like this.

2 Glue the other two bumps upside-down in the middle holes. Cut out and glue paper teeth to the jaws.

3 Cut holes in the back for two fingers and a thumb.

You will need: a papier mâché egg box, scissors, glue, tissue
or crepe paper.

Cut out and glue
on paper eyelashes.

4

Glue tissue or crepe
paper inside the mouth.
Make the long paper
tongue hang out.
If there is a tab here,
cut it into teeth.

5

Put your
fingers in
the holes
and pin a
cloth round
your hand.

Paint the
face a bright
colour with
dark dots,
and the eyes
white with
black centres.

FINGER MICE

1

To make two mice: draw around a saucer on a piece of felt.

Cut the circle in half. Cut one half into two – these are the bodies. Cut the other half into three pieces. Use two of them for cone shaped heads. Mark the third piece with coins for the back of the head and ears, like this.

2

Cut out this shape and a strip along the edge for arms. Repeat this piece on a scrap of felt.

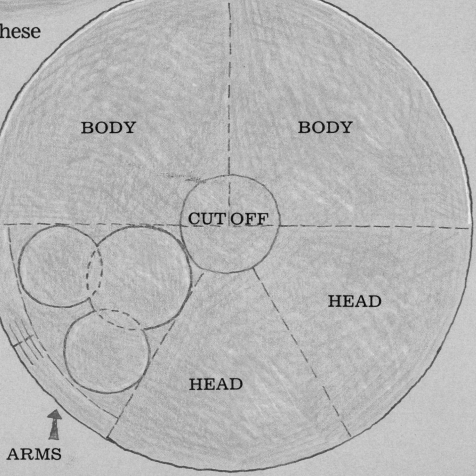

BODY

BODY

CUT OFF

HEAD

HEAD

ARMS

You will need: a piece of felt (15cm × 15cm) or scraps of various colours, scissors, needle and cotton, small beads, cotton wool.

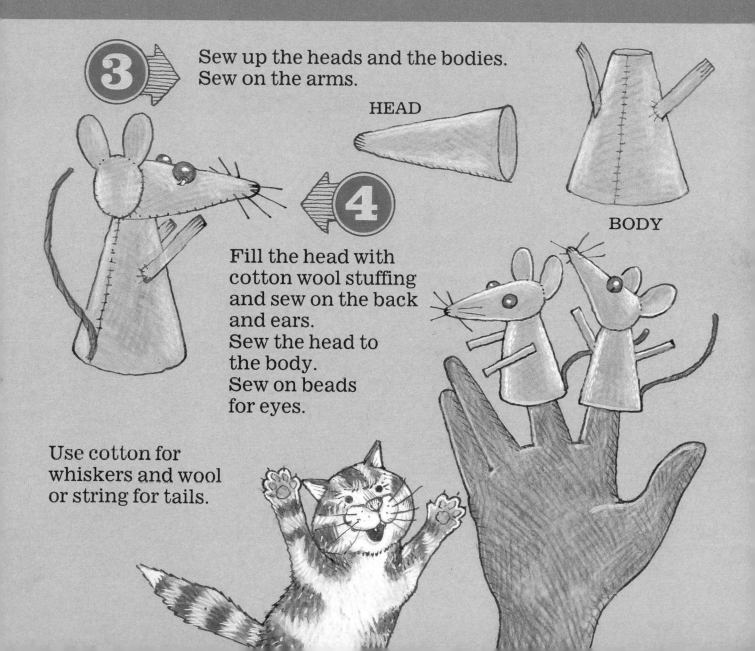

3 Sew up the heads and the bodies. Sew on the arms.

HEAD

BODY

4 Fill the head with cotton wool stuffing and sew on the back and ears.
Sew the head to the body.
Sew on beads for eyes.

Use cotton for whiskers and wool or string for tails.

OLD GLOVE OWL A glove puppet

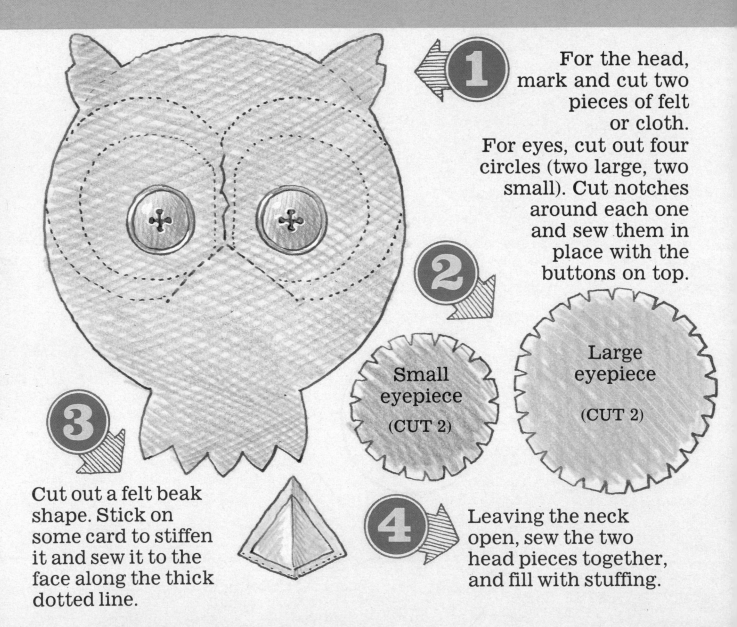

1 For the head, mark and cut two pieces of felt or cloth. For eyes, cut out four circles (two large, two small). Cut notches around each one and sew them in place with the buttons on top.

2

Small eyepiece

(CUT 2)

Large eyepiece

(CUT 2)

3 Cut out a felt beak shape. Stick on some card to stiffen it and sew it to the face along the thick dotted line.

4 Leaving the neck open, sew the two head pieces together, and fill with stuffing.

You will need: some pieces of coloured felt or cloth, scissors, two buttons, needle and cotton, stuffing or cotton wool, an old glove.

5 Using this shape, cut six pieces of felt or cloth for the wings and body.

6 Put on the glove and poke your first two fingers up into the head. Sew the owl to the glove, leaving room for your fingers.

7 Sew the body and wing pieces to the glove.

SNAPPY CROCODILE A sleeve puppet

1 Cut the sleeve from an old jersey or make a cloth tube. Push newspaper into it.

Cut the bumps off an egg tray and glue them to the sleeve in three rows of four.
Leave to dry with a weight on top. This is the body.

25cm

2 Cut a tea packet diagonally into two. Cut a square out of the large ends.

3 Glue two matchbox covers into the large ends. For the jaw hinge, cut a strip of felt and glue it to join the two halves. Leave a gap of about 5cm between them.

You will need: an old sleeve or tube of cloth, newspaper,
a papier mâché egg box, scissors, glue,
a tea packet or similar box, two empty
matchboxes, a piece of felt, string, paint.

4 ⇨ Fold the two halves together.
Glue on pieces of egg box as
eyes. Cut teeth along the
edges. Glue the head to the
body. Thread pieces of egg
box on a string for the tail.

⇦ **5** Sew on legs made out of the
remaining pieces of sleeve.

Paint the
crocodile.

FROG ON A LILY PAD

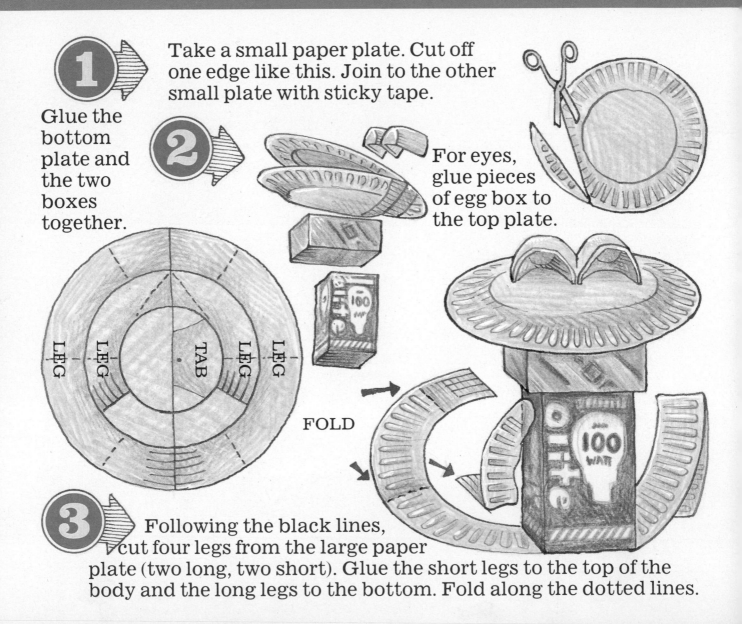

1 Take a small paper plate. Cut off one edge like this. Join to the other small plate with sticky tape.

Glue the bottom plate and the two boxes together.

2 For eyes, glue pieces of egg box to the top plate.

FOLD

LEG LEG LEG TAB LEG LEG

3 Following the black lines, cut four legs from the large paper plate (two long, two short). Glue the short legs to the top of the body and the long legs to the bottom. Fold along the dotted lines.

4 ➤

Glue a tab to the base of the frog's back and join it to the head with a pipe cleaner.

Glue the body and legs to another large pad for the lily pond. Paint the whole frog.

5 ➤

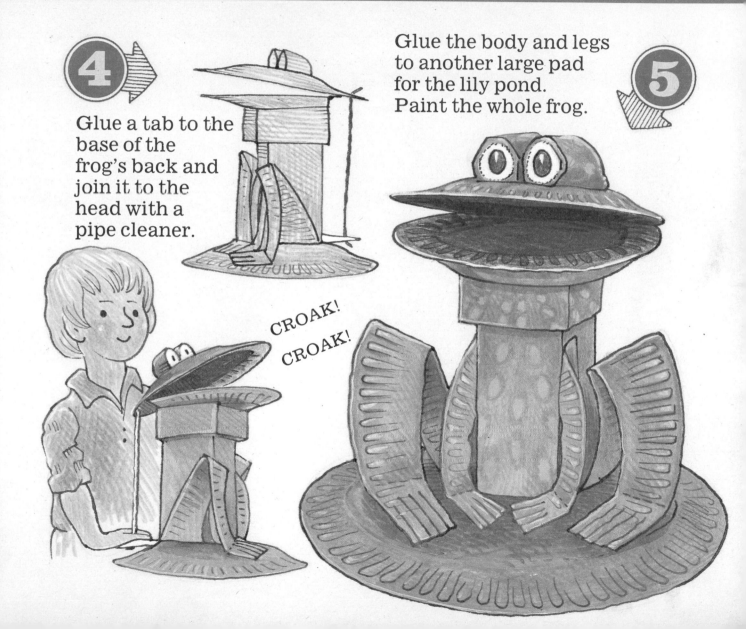

CROAK!

CROAK!

SPOTTY SPIDER A string puppet

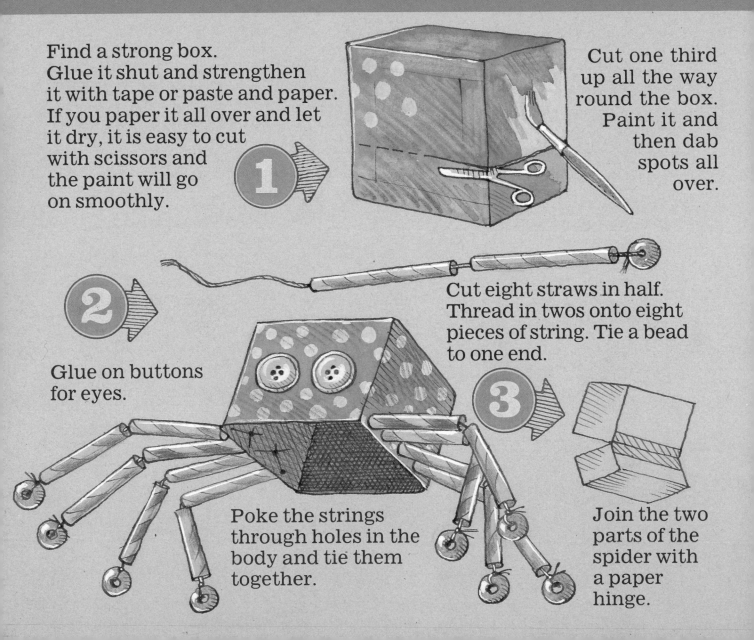

Find a strong box.
Glue it shut and strengthen
it with tape or paste and paper.
If you paper it all over and let
it dry, it is easy to cut
with scissors and
the paint will go
on smoothly.

1

Cut one third
up all the way
round the box.
Paint it and
then dab
spots all
over.

2

Glue on buttons
for eyes.

Cut eight straws in half.
Thread in twos onto eight
pieces of string. Tie a bead
to one end.

3

Poke the strings
through holes in the
body and tie them
together.

Join the two
parts of the
spider with
a paper
hinge.

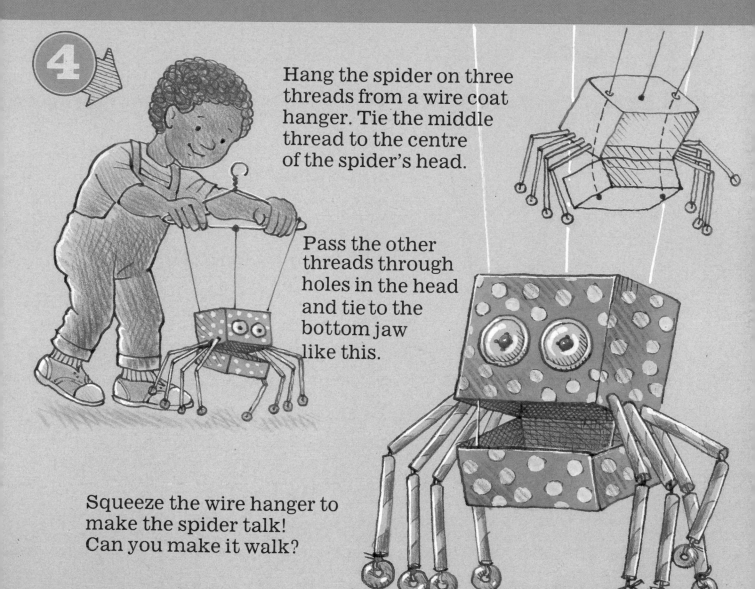

You will need: a strong square box, glue, tape or paper, scissors, paint, eight straws, string or thin thread, eight straws, eight beads, two buttons, a wire coat hanger.

4

Hang the spider on three threads from a wire coat hanger. Tie the middle thread to the centre of the spider's head.

Pass the other threads through holes in the head and tie to the bottom jaw like this.

Squeeze the wire hanger to make the spider talk! Can you make it walk?

ROB ROBOT A string puppet

1 Use the smaller box to make a painted head with a hinged jaw as for the spider.

2 Using the film cans, mark and cut out four holes; two in the front for eyes, and two in the top. Push the four film cans through the holes and fix at the back with tape.

Fix a toilet roll tube for a neck.

Use film cans or cotton reels on rubber bands for arms. Keep them in place with twisted pipe cleaners.

3 Paint the larger box. Cut a square hole in the back of both boxes. Cut a round hole in the top of the big box for the neck. Push in the toilet roll tube and secure with a straw.

You will need: two large boxes (such as soap powder or wine boxes), scissors, plastic film cans, toilet roll tubes, a straw, cotton reels, pipe cleaners, an egg box, a wire coat hanger.

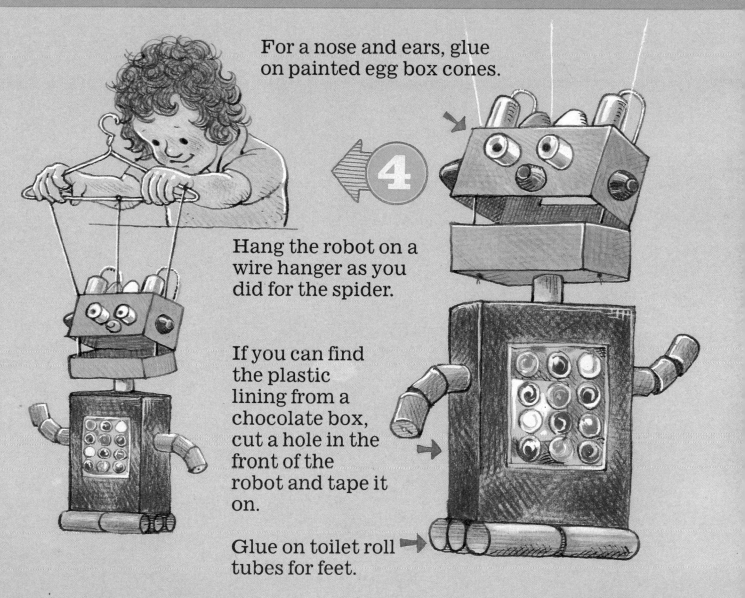

For a nose and ears, glue on painted egg box cones.

4

Hang the robot on a wire hanger as you did for the spider.

If you can find the plastic lining from a chocolate box, cut a hole in the front of the robot and tape it on.

Glue on toilet roll tubes for feet.